THE GREAT PHILOSOPHERS

Consulting Editors
Ray Monk and Frederic Raphael

TURING

Andrew Hodges

ROUTLEDGE
New York

Published in 1999 by
Routledge
29 West 35th Street
New York, NY 10001

First published in 1997 by
Phoenix
A Division of the Orion Publishing Group Ltd.
Orion House
5 Upper Saint Martin's Lane
London WC2H 9EA

10 9 8 7 6 5 4 3 2 1

Library of Congress Cataloging-in-Publication Data

Hodges, Andrew.
        Turing / Andrew Hodges.
          p. cm.—(The great philosophers : 3)
        Includes bibliographical references.
        ISBN 0-415-92378-6 (pbk.)
        1. Turing, Alan Mathison, 1912–1954. 2. Artificial
        intelligence. 3. Mathemeticians—Great Britain
        Biography. I. Title. II. Series: Great Philosophers
        (Routledge (Firm)) : 3.
QA29.T8H632 1999
510'.92—dc21   99-22485
                                                    CIP

ACKNOWLEDGEMENTS

I am grateful for the specific permission to include extended extracts from Alan Turing's writings. The Turing Estate has kindly allowed the quotation of passages from Turing's unpublished writings. The extracts from the papers of 1936 and 1939 appear by permission of the London Mathematical Society. The National Physical Laboratory reports of 1946 and 1948 are Crown Copyright and are reproduced by permission of the Controller of HMSO. The extracts from the Mind article of 1950 appear by permission of Oxford University Press. The Turing –Wittgenstein dialogue appears by permission of Harvester Wheatsheaf.

TURING

A Natural Philosopher

INTRODUCTION

Alan Turing dared to ask whether a machine could think. His contributions to understanding and answering this and other questions defy conventional classification. At the close of the twentieth century, the 1936 concept of the Turing machine appears not only in mathematics and computer science, but in cognitive science and theoretical biology. His 1950 paper 'Computing machinery and intelligence', describing the so-called Turing test, is a cornerstone of the theory of artificial intelligence. In between, Turing played a vital role in the outcome of the Second World War, and produced single-handedly a far-sighted plan for the construction and use of an electronic computer. He thought and lived a generation ahead of his time, and yet the features of his thought that burst the boundaries of the 1940s are better described by the antique words: *natural philosophy*.

Alan Turing's immersion in and attack upon Nature was a unity; divisions between mathematics, science, technology and philosophy in his work have tended to obscure his ideas. He was not a prolific author; much remained unpublished in his lifetime; some remained secret into the 1990s. Private communications shed a little more light on the development of his thought, a subject on which he was generally silent. We shall see, for instance, how he came to logic and computation from a youthful fascination with the physical description of mind. But we have only hints as to the formation of his convictions amidst the secrecy of wartime cryptanalysis, and suggestions of fresh ideas are lost in the drama of his mysterious death.

THE NATURE OF TURING'S WORLD

Alan Mathison Turing was born in London on 23 June 1912, and from the beginning showed a personality out of place in the upper-middle-class schooling undergone by sons of Indian Civil Service officers. Conformity to class meant unquestioning obedience to the rituals of the British preparatory and public school. But the book *Natural Wonders Every Child Should Know* opened his eyes to the concept of scientific explanation, and from then on Nature as opposed to human convention commanded his attention, as many nagging reports demonstrated. Duty, hierarchy, masters, servants, rules and games would later play a striking role in the illustration of his ideas; but while at school he was more baffled and incompetent than rebellious at the demands of the British empire, ignoring as much as possible while pursuing his own priorities. In 1925 he wrote to his mother: 'I am making a collection of experiments in the order I mean to do them in. I always seem to want to make things from the thing that is commonest in nature and with the least waste in energy.'[1]

His experimental chemistry incurred displeasure, as did poor handwriting and unconventional methods in his mathematics. He was bottom of the form in English. The headmaster wrote, 'If he is to stay at a Public School, he must aim at becoming *educated*. If he is to be solely a Scientific Specialist, he is wasting his time at a Public School' and this judgment on British ruling-class priorities was almost correct. Turing was nearly prevented from taking the equivalent of GCSEs. Thereafter, he found his level in Einstein's own exposition of relativity and Eddington's view of quantum mechanics in *The Nature of the Physical World*. But this was isolated private study, and he

4

might never have felt the urge to communicate but for an impossibly romantic story.

Human nature brought him to life; but it was his own homosexual nature, bringing revelation and trauma in equal measure. He fell in unrequited love with Christopher Morcom, a very talented youth in the school sixth form, and his longing for friendship brought him to communicate. A brief flowering of scientific collaboration perished when Morcom suddenly died in February 1930. Turing's correspondence with the dead boy's mother gives insight into the development of his ideas in the aftermath. He was concerned to believe the dead boy could still exist in spirit, and to reconcile such a belief with science. To this end he wrote for Mrs Morcom an essay, probably in 1932. It is the private writing of a twenty-year-old, and must be read as testament to background and not as a thesis upheld in public; nevertheless it is a key to Turing's future development.

Nature of Spirit

It used to be supposed in Science that if everything was known about the Universe at any particular moment then we can predict what it will be through all the future ... More modern science however has come to the conclusion that when we are dealing with atoms and electrons we are quite unable to know the exact state of them; our instruments being made of atoms and electrons themselves. The conception then of being able to know the exact state of the universe then must really break down on the small scale. This means that the theory which held that as eclipses etc. are predestined so were all our actions breaks down too. We have a will which is able to determine the action of the atoms probably in a small portion of the brain, or possibly all over it. The rest of the body acts so as to amplify this ... [2]

In stating the classic paradox of physical determinism

and free will, Turing is influenced by Eddington's assertion that quantum mechanical physics ('more modern science') yields room for human will. Eddington asked how could 'this collection of ordinary atoms be a thinking machine?' and Turing tries to find some answer. His essay goes on to espouse belief in a spirit unconstrained by the body: 'when the body dies the "mechanism" of the body, holding the spirit is gone and the spirit finds a new body sooner or later perhaps immediately.' Letters show he retained such ideas at least until 1933.

Turing was much more successful in undergraduate work than at school, and King's College lent him a protective ambience sympathetic to homosexuality and unconventional opinion. He was not, however, one of its élite social circle, nor in a political group. Politically, he responded briefly to the 1933 anti-war movement, but not to the Communist party as others of his close acquaintance did. Nor did Turing share the pacifism of his first lover, fellow mathematics student James Atkins.

In a similar way Turing found a home in Cambridge mathematical culture, yet did not belong entirely to it. The division between 'pure' and 'applied' mathematics was at Cambridge then as now very strong, but Turing ignored it, and he never showed mathematical parochialism. If anything, it was the attitude of a Russell that he acquired, assuming that mastery of so difficult a subject granted the right to invade others. Turing showed little intellectual diffidence once in his stride: in March 1933 he acquired Russell's *Introduction to Mathematical Philosophy*, and on 1 December 1933, the philosopher R. B. Braithwaite minuted in the Moral Science Club records: 'A. M. Turing read a paper on "Mathematics and logic". He suggested that a purely logistic view of mathematics was inadequate; and that mathematical propositions possessed a variety of interpretations, of which the logistic was merely one.' At the same time he was studying von Neumann's 1932 *Grundlagen den Quantenmechanik*. Thus, it may be that

Eddington's claims for quantum mechanics had encouraged the shift of Turing's interest towards logical foundations. And it was logic that made Alan Turing's name.

THE TURING MACHINE AND THE ENTSCHEIDUNGSPROBLEM

When, in the spring of 1935, Turing attended the advanced lectures on the Foundations of Mathematics given by the Cambridge topologist M. H. A. Newman, he was not making a career move. Mathematical logic was a small, abstruse, technically difficult area devoid of applications, and unrepresented in the undergraduate curriculum. Turing's work was a labour of love.

Newman's lectures brought Turing to the point reached by Gödel in his now-famous 1931 Incompleteness theorem. The underlying problem here addressed is how we can grasp the truth of a statement about *infinitely many* instances: such as that for all, a, b, c, $(a+b) \times c = a \times c + b \times c$, or that there is no largest prime number. An apparently reasonable response might be that statements such as these do not in fact involve infinitely many instances at all, but are only finite sentences with words like 'all' in them, deduced by finitely many rules of deductive logic. Mathematical logicians in the late nineteenth century had tried to make this argument explicit, but Bertrand Russell, showing how finite descriptions like 'set of all sets' could be self-contradictory, had discovered the unavoidable difficulties that arose through *self-referential* terms. Since then the mathematician David Hilbert had made more precise demands of any proposed finite scheme in the famous terms: consistency, completeness and decidability. In 1931 Gödel had shown that consistency and completeness could not both be attained: there were statements about numbers, indubitably true, which could not be proved from finite axioms by finitely many rules. Gödel's proof rested on the idea that statements *about* numbers could be coded *as* numbers, and constructing a self-referential statement to defeat Hilbert's hopes.

Gödel's work left outstanding Hilbert's question of *decidability*, the *Entscheidungsproblem*, namely the question of whether there exists a definite method which, at least in principle, can be applied to a given proposition to decide whether that proposition is provable. In a restricted calculus there may indeed be such a method: for example, the truth-table technique for deciding whether a formula in elementary propositional logic is a tautology. Could there be such a decision procedure for mathematical propositions? This question had survived Gödel's analysis because its settlement required a precise and convincing definition of *method*. Giving precise definitions is the meat and drink of pure mathematics, but in this case, something more than precision was called for – it had to be something unassailable in its generality, which would not be superseded by a more powerful class of methods. There had, in fact, to be some philosophical as well as some mathematical analysis.

This, working by himself for the year until April 1936, Turing achieved; his idea, now known as the *Turing machine*, was to be published at the very end of 1936 in a paper 'On computable numbers, with an application to the *Entscheidungsproblem.*'[3] It is characteristic of Turing that he refreshed Hilbert's question by casting it in terms not of proofs, but of computing *numbers*. The reformulation staked a clearer claim to have found an idea central to mathematics. As his title said, the *Entscheidungsproblem* was only an application of a new idea, that of computability. There are no surviving drafts or correspondence relating to its formation; no later accounts of his intellectual journey; just the story he told to his later student Robin Gandy that he had the main idea while lying in Grantchester meadows. Newman only saw the work when it was fully formed.

His paper starts with the line of thought already mentioned: how can we specify the infinite in finite terms? In particular, how can we specify the infinite sequence of digits in a 'real number', such as $\pi = 3.141592653 \ldots$? What does it mean to say that there is a definite method for calculating such a number? Turing's answer lies in defining the concept of the Turing machine.

> We may compare a man in the process of computing a real number to a machine which is only capable of a finite number of conditions … which will be called 'm-configurations'. The machine is supplied with a 'tape' (the analogue of paper) running through it, and divided into sections (called 'squares') each capable of bearing a 'symbol'. At any moment there is just one square … which is 'in the machine'. We may call this square the 'scanned square'. The symbol on the scanned square may be called the 'scanned symbol'. The 'scanned symbol' is the only one of which the machine is, so to speak, 'directly aware' …

Turing then specifies precisely the repertoire of action available to the imagined machine. The action is totally determined by the 'configuration' it is in, and the symbol it is currently scanning. It is this complete determination that makes it 'a machine'. The action is limited to the following: at each step it (1) either erases the symbol or prints a specified symbol; (2) moves one square either to left or right; (3) changes to a new configuration.

Slightly different versions of Turing's idea are given in different textbooks, and the precise technical form he originally gave is not important; the essence is that the action is completely given by what Turing calls a 'table of behaviour' for the machine, dictating what it will do for every configuration and every symbol scanned. Each 'table of behaviour' is a different Turing machine.

The actions are highly restricted in form, but Turing's

thesis is that they form a set of atomic elements out of which all mathematical operations can be composed. In fact, in a style most unusual for a mathematical paper, argument is given in very general terms, justifying the Turing machine actions as sufficient to encompass the most general possible method:

> Computing is normally done by writing certain symbols on paper. We may suppose this paper is divided into squares like a child's arithmetic book. In elementary arithmetic the two-dimensional character of the paper is sometimes used. But such a use is always avoidable, and I think that it will be agreed that the two-dimensional character of paper is no essential of computation. I assume then that the computation is carried out on one-dimensional paper, *i.e.* on a tape divided into squares. I shall also suppose that the number of symbols which may be printed is finite. If we were to allow an infinity of symbols, then there would be symbols differing to an arbitrarily small extent. [A footnote gives a topological argument for this.] The effect of this restriction of the number of symbols is not very serious. It is always possible to use sequences of symbols in the place of single symbols … This is in accordance with experience. We cannot tell at a glance whether 9999999999999999 and 999999999999999 are the same.

Turing thus claims that a finite repertoire of symbols actually allows a countable infinity of symbols, but not an infinity of *immediately recognisable* symbols. Note that the tape also has to be of unlimited length, although at any time the number of symbols on it is finite. In the next paragraph note that the word 'computer' then meant a *person* doing computing. Turing's model is that of a *human mind* at work.

> The behaviour of the computer at any moment is determined by the symbols which he is observing, and

his 'state of mind' at that moment. We may suppose that there is a bound B to the number of symbols or squares which the computer can observe at one moment. If he wishes to observe more, he must use successive observations. We will also suppose that the number of states of mind which need to be taken into account is finite. The reasons for this are of the same character as those which restrict the number of symbols. If we admitted an infinity of states of mind, some of them will be 'arbitrarily close' and will be confused. Again, the restriction is not one which seriously affects computation, since the use of more complicated states of mind can be avoided by writing more symbols on the tape.

Let us imagine the operations performed by the computer to be split up into 'simple operations' which are so elementary that it is not easy to imagine them further divided. Every such operation consists of some change of the physical system consisting of the computer and his tape. We know the state of the system if we know the sequence of symbols on the tape, which of these are observed by the computer (possibly with a special order), and the state of mind of the computer. We may suppose that in a simple operation not more than one symbol is altered. Any other changes can be split up into simple changes of this kind. The situation in regard to the squares whose symbols may be altered in this way is the same as in regard to the observed squares. We may, therefore, without loss of generality, assume that the squares whose symbols are changed are always 'observed' squares.

Besides these changes of symbols, the simple operations must include changes of distribution of observed squares. The new observed squares must be immediately recognisable by the computer. I think it is reasonable to suppose that they can only be squares whose distance

11

from the closest of the immediately previously observed squares does not exceed a certain fixed amount. Let us say that each of the new observed squares is within L squares of an immediately previously observed square.

In connection with 'immediate recognisability', it may be thought that there are other kinds of square which are immediately recognisable. In particular, squares marked by special symbols might be taken as immediately recognisable. Now if these squares are marked only by single symbols there can be only a finite number of them, and we should not upset our theory by adjoining these marked squares to the observed squares. If, however, they are marked by a sequence of symbols, we cannot regard the process of recognition as a simple process. This is a fundamental point and should be illustrated. In most mathematical papers the equations and theorems are numbered. Normally the numbers do not go beyond (say) 1000. It is, therefore, possible to recognise a theorem at a glance by its number. But if the paper was very long, we might reach Theorem 157767733443477; then, further on in the paper, we might find '... hence (applying Theorem 157767733443477) we have ...'. In order to make sure which was the relevant theorem we should have to compare the two numbers figure by figure ...

The simple operations must therefore include:

(a) Changes of the symbol on one of the observed squares.
(b) Changes of one of the squares observed to another square within L squares of one of the previously observed squares.

It may be that some of these changes necessarily involve a change of state of mind. The most general single operation must therefore be taken to be one of the following:

(A) A possible change (a) of symbol together with a possible change of state of mind.

(B) A possible change (b) of observed squares, together with a possible change of state of mind.

The operation actually performed is determined, as has been suggested [above], by the state of mind of the computer and the observed symbols. In particular, they determine the state of mind of the computer after the operation is carried out.

Turing now continues, 'We may now construct a machine to do the work of this computer' – that is, specify a Turing machine to do the work of this human calculator. Note, for its later significance, that Turing does not here raise the question of whether the mind is capable of actions which can *not* be described as computations.

Turing was very bold and untypical of mathematicians in placing this analysis of mental activity at the forefront. He added a less contentious argument:

… we avoid introducing the 'state of mind' by considering a more physical and definite counterpart of it. It is always possible for the computer to break off from his work, to go away and forget all about it, and later to come back and go on with it. If he does this he must leave a note of instructions (written in some standard form) explaining how the work is to be continued. This note is the counterpart of the 'state of mind'. We will suppose that the computer works in such a desultory manner that he never does more than one step at a sitting. The note of instructions must enable him to carry out one step and write the next note. Thus the state of progress of the computation at any one stage is completely determined by the note of instructions and the symbols on the tape …

But note that this calls for the method to be *consciously*

known in every detail, whereas the 'state of mind' argument could be held to apply to a person who can reliably perform a process without being able to describe it explicitly.

The *computable numbers* are then defined as those infinite decimals which can be printed by a Turing machine starting with a blank tape. He sketches a proof that π is a computable number, along with every real number defined by the ordinary methods of equation and limits in mathematical work. But armed with this new definition, it is now easy to show that *uncomputable* numbers exist. The crucial point is that the table of behaviour of any Turing machine is *finite*. Hence, all the possible tables of behaviour can be listed in an alphabetical order: this shows that the computable numbers are countable. Since the real numbers are uncountable, it follows that *almost all* of them are uncomputable. We can refine this idea to exhibit a particular uncomputable number. Before showing the construction, a point has to be noted: a table of behaviour may have the property of running in a loop and never producing more than a finite number of digits.

With this in mind, we again place all Turing machines in an alphabetical order of their tables in behaviour. We discard those which fail to produce an infinite series of digits, leaving only the Turing machines which produce infinite strings of digits – the computable numbers. Let us suppose that binary notation is being used, so that the digits are either 0 or 1. Now define a new number so that its nth digit is different from the nth digit produced by the nth machine. This new number differs in at least one place from every computable number; therefore it cannot be computable.

As Turing explains, this seems to be a paradox. If it can be described finitely, why can it not be computed? Inspection shows that the problem comes in identifying those Turing machines which fail to produce infinitely many digits. This is *not* a computable operation: that is, there is no Turing

14

machine which can inspect the table of any other machine and decide whether it will produce infinitely many digits or not. This can be seen more directly: if there *were* such a machine, it could be applied to itself, and this idea can be used to get a contradiction. Nowadays this is known as the fact that the *halting problem* cannot be decided by a Turing machine. From this discovery of a problem that cannot be decided by a machine, it is not a difficult step to employ the formal calculus of mathematical logic, and to answer Hilbert's *Entscheidungsproblem* in the negative.

A point which Turing stressed, however, is that there is no inconsistency involved in *defining* uncomputable numbers; in modern computability theory they are the subject of rigorous manipulation and logical argument. It may even be that every digit of an uncomputable number may be calculated; the point is, however, that infinitely many different methods are required to work them out. Nevertheless the property of computability rests on mathematical bedrock: this was Turing's claim at the time and it has never since been challenged.

CHURCH'S THESIS AND TURING'S THESIS

This was a triumph for anyone, let alone an isolated graduate of twenty-three, but Turing suffered an immediate setback in a tiresomely classic case of scientific coincidence. Before he had submitted his paper, Alonzo Church, the pre-eminent American logician at Princeton, announced the same conclusion regarding the *Entscheidungsproblem*. Turing took the time until August 1936 to write an appendix relating his result to Church's. For publication by the London Mathematical Society, Newman had to make a case that Turing's argument was different from that produced by Church. In fact Turing's argument differed from Church's in a fundamental way. When the dust had settled, in 1938, he gave his own view in the self-effacing terms that in public he always used of his own work:

A function is said to be 'effectively calculable' if its values can be found by some purely mechanical process. Although it is fairly easy to get an intuitive grasp of this idea, it is nevertheless desirable to have some more definite, mathematically expressible definition. Such a definition was first given by Gödel at Princeton in 1934 ... These functions were described as 'general recursive' by Gödel ... Another definition of effective calculability has been given by Church ... who identifies it with λ-definability. The author [i.e. Turing himself] has recently suggested a definition corresponding more closely to the intuitive idea ... It was stated above that 'a function is effectively calculable if its values can be found by some purely mechanical process.' We may take this statement literally, understanding by a purely mechanical process one which could be carried out by a machine ... The development of these ideas leads to the author's definition of a computable function, and to an identification of computability [in Turing's precise technical sense] with effective calculability. It is not difficult, though somewhat laborious, to prove that these three definitions are equivalent.[4]

Turing here gives a view on what is now known and famous as *Church's thesis*. Although Church's thesis is nowadays given various other interpretations, in 1936 it was the claim that effective calculability could be identified with the operations of Church's very elegant and surprising formalism, that of the *lambda-calculus*. As such it lay *within* the world of mathematical formalism. But Turing offers a reason *why Church's thesis should be true*, drawing on ideas *external* to mathematics such as that one cannot do see or choose between more than a finite number of things at one time. Church's thesis is now sometimes called the Church-Turing thesis, but the Turing thesis is different, bringing the physical world into the picture with a claim of what can be done. It should not go without mention that Turing after referring to his machine definition of computability, also cited the work of the Polish-American logician Emil Post, which had also brought an idea of physical action into computation. However Post had not developed his ideas so fully.

THE UNIVERSAL TURING MACHINE

Since the modern digital *computer* is now so important to the exploration of Turing's ideas, a digression is called for to explain its relationship to this paper. It is a startling fact that 'On computable numbers' not only solved a major outstanding question posed by Hilbert, opened the new mathematical field of computability, and offered a new analysis of mental activity, but had a practical implication: it laid out the principle of the computer through the concept of the universal Turing machine.

The idea of the universal machine is easily indicated. Once the specification of any Turing machine is given as a table of behaviour, tracing the operation of that machine becomes a mechanical matter of looking up entries in the table. Because it is mechanical, a Turing machine can do it: that is, a single Turing machine may be designed to have the property that, when supplied with the table of behaviour of another Turing machine, it will do what that other Turing machine would have done. Turing called such a machine the universal machine. A technical problem arises in encoding the table in a linear form for the 'tape' and arranging working space, but these are details.

Turing introduced the universal machine as a tool in the argument described above for exhibiting an uncomputable number. As such it was not necessary to his conclusion regarding the *Entscheidungsproblem*. But Turing made the very striking concept prominent in his paper, and according to Newman's later statement, was inspired *even then* to consider practical construction. It is the universal machine which gives Turing the claim to have invented the principle of the computer – and not merely in abstract principle, as we shall see. And nowadays it is impossible to study Turing machines without thinking of them as computer programs, with the universal machine as the computer on which the programs are run. It is not difficult to turn a 'table of behaviour' into the explicit form of a modern program, in which each 'configuration' becomes a numbered instruction, containing IF conditions which dictate a writing action and the number of the next instruction.

Some care is needed here with terminology. The phrase 'the Turing machine' is analogous to 'the printed book' in referring to a class of potentially infinitely many examples. Within this class, certain Turing machines are 'universal', having sufficient complexity to interpret and execute the table of behaviour of any other Turing machine. Again, although we speak of 'the' universal Turing machine, there are infinitely many designs with this property.

Turing's own work in constructing tables of behaviour must have put him in the mind of a programmer; all the more so as Turing used abbreviated notation which amounts to defining subroutines. The mind of the programmer cannot be said to originate with Turing's paper; the axiomatic programme, and Gödel's ingenious methods, had already given rise to this way of thinking. But in Turing's work the idea is formalised in the language of instruction, to a degree that it is hard to believe that the computer was not already in existence. Yet the point should be emphasised: Turing was *not* considering the computing machines of his day. He was modelling the action of human minds. The physical machines would come ten years later.

THINKING THE UNCOMPUTABLE

Turing then studied at Princeton for two academic years, with a break back at Cambridge in summer 1937. It was a period of intense activity at a world centre of mathematics. Turing was over-optimistic in thinking he could rewrite the foundations of analysis, and added nothing to the remarks about limits and convergence given in 'Computable numbers'. (One reason for this might be the following: if x and y are computable numbers, as specified as Turing machines, the truth of the statements $x=y$, or $x=0$ cannot tested by a computable process.) But besides wide-ranging research in analysis, topology and algebra, and the 'laborious' work of showing the equivalence of his definition of computability to those of Church and Gödel, he extended the exploration of the logic of mental activity with a paper 'Systems of logic based on ordinals'.[5]

This, his most difficult paper, is much less well known than his definition of computability. It is generally regarded as a diversion from his line of thought on computability, computers and the philosophy of mind, and I fell into this assumption in *Alan Turing: the Enigma* (see Further Reading), essentially because I followed Turing's own later standpoint. But I now consider that *at the time*, Turing saw himself steaming straight ahead with the analysis of the mind, by studying a question complementary to 'On computable numbers'. Turing asked in this paper whether it is possible to formalize those actions of the mind which are *not* those of following a definite method: mental actions one might call creative or original in nature. In particular,

Turing focused on the action of seeing the truth of one of Gödel's unprovable assertions.

Gödel had shown that when we see the truth of an unprovable proposition, we cannot be doing so by following given rules. The rules may be augmented so as to bring this particular proposition into their ambit, but then there will be yet another true proposition that is not captured by the new rules of proof, and so on *ad infinitum*. The question arises as to to whether there is some higher type of rule which can organise this process of 'Gödelisation'. An *ordinal logic* is such a rule, based on the theory of *ordinal numbers*, the very rich and subtle theory of different ways in which an infinite number of entities may be placed in sequence. An ordinal logic turns the idea of 'and so on *ad infinitum*' into a precise formulation. Turing wrote that: 'The purpose of introducing ordinal logics is to avoid as far as possible the effects of Gödel's theorem.' The uncomputable could not be made computable, but ordinal logics would bring it into as much order as was possible.

Turing's work, in which he proved important (though somewhat negative) results about such logical schemes, founded a new area of mathematical logic. But the motivation, as he himself stated it, was in mental philosophy. As in 'On computable numbers', he was unafraid of using psychological terms, this time the word 'intuition' appearing for the act of recognising the truth of an unprovable Gödel sentence:

> Mathematical reasoning may be regarded rather schematically as combination of two faculties, which we may call *intuition* and *ingenuity*. The activity of the intuition consists in making spontaneous judgments which are not the result of conscious trains of reasoning. These judgments are often but by no means invariably correct (leaving aside the question what is meant by 'correct'). Often it is possible to find some other way of verifying the correctness of an intuitive judgment. We may, for

instance, judge that all positive integers are uniquely factorizable into primes; a detailed mathematical argument leads to the same result. This argument will also involve intuitive judgments, but they will be less open to criticism than the original judgment about factorization. I shall not attempt to explain this idea of 'intuition' any more explicitly.

The exercise of ingenuity in mathematics consists in aiding the intuition through suitable arrangements of propositions, and perhaps geometrical figures or drawings. It is intended that when these are really well arranged the validity of the intuitive steps which are required cannot seriously be doubted.

Turing then explains how the axiomatisation of mathematics was originally intended to eliminate all intuition, but Gödel had shown that to be impossible. The Turing machine construction had shown how to make all formal proofs 'mechanical'; and in the present paper such mechanical operations were to be taken as trivial, instead putting under the microscope the non-mechanical steps which remained.

In consequence of the impossibility of finding a formal logic which wholly eliminates the necessity of using intuition, we naturally turn to 'non-constructive' systems of logic with which not all the steps in a proof are mechanical, some being intuitive. An example of a non-constructive logic is afforded by any ordinal logic ... What properties do we desire a non-constructive logic to have if we are to make use of it for the expression of mathematical proofs? We want it to show quite clearly when a step makes use of intuition, and when it is purely formal. The strain put on the intuition should be a minimum. Most important of all, it must be beyond doubt that the logic leads to correct results whenever the intuitive steps are correct.

It is not clear how literally Turing meant the identification with 'intuition' to be taken. Probably his ideas were fluid, and he added a cautionary footnote: 'We are leaving out of account that most important faculty which distinguishes topics of interest from others; in fact we are regarding the function of the mathematician as simply to determine the truth or falsity of propositions.' But the evidence is that at this time he was open to the idea that in moments of 'intuition' the mind appears to do something outside the scope of the Turing machine. If so, he was not alone: Gödel and Post held this view.

TURING AND WITTGENSTEIN

As it happened, Turing's views were probed by the leading philosopher of the time at just this point. Unfortunately their recorded conversations shed no light upon Turing's view of mind and machine. Turing was introduced to Wittgenstein in summer 1937, and when Turing returned to Cambridge for the autumn term of 1938, he attended Wittgenstein's lectures – more a Socratic discussion group – on the Foundations of Mathematics. These were noted by the participants and have been reconstructed and published.[6] There is a curious similarity of the style of speech – plain speaking and argument by question and answer – but they were on different wavelengths. In a dialogue at the heart of the sequence they debated the significance of axiomatising mathematics and the problems that had arisen in doing so:

Wittgenstein: ... Think of the case of the Liar. It is very queer in a way that this should have puzzled anyone – much more extraordinary than you might think ... Because the thing works like this: if a man says 'I am lying' we say that it follows that he is not lying, from which it follows that he is lying and so on. Well, so what? You can go on like that until you are black in the face. Why not? It doesn't matter. ... it is just a useless language-game, and why should anybody be excited?

Turing: What puzzles one is that one usually uses a contradiction as a criterion for having done something wrong. But in this case one cannot find anything done wrong.

W: Yes – and more: nothing has been done wrong. ... where will the harm come?

T: The real harm will not come in unless there is an application, in which a bridge may fall down or something of that sort.

W: ... The question is: Why are people afraid of contradictions? It is easy to understand why they should be afraid of contradictions, etc., *outside* mathematics. The question is: Why should they be afraid of contradictions inside mathematics? Turing says, 'Because something may go wrong with the application.' But nothing need go wrong. And if something does go wrong – if the bridge breaks down – then your mistake was of the kind of using a wrong natural law ...

T: You cannot be confident about applying your calculus until you know that there is no hidden contradiction in it.

W: There seems to me an enormous mistake there. ... Suppose I convince Rhees of the paradox of the Liar, and he says, 'I lie, therefore I do not lie, therefore I lie and I do not lie, therefore we have a contradiction, therefore 2 × 2 = 369.' Well, we should not call this 'multiplication', that is all ...

T: Although you do not know that the bridge will fall if there are no contradictions, yet it is almost certain that if there are contradictions it will go wrong somewhere.

W: But nothing has ever gone wrong that way yet ...

Turing's responses reflect mainstream mathematical

thought and practice, rather than showing his distinctive characteristics and original ideas. In 1938, it should be noted, he was an untenured research fellow whose first application for a lectureship had failed, and whose chance of a conventional career lay in the mathematics studied and taught at Cambridge. His work in logic was but a part of his output, by no means well known. His fellowship was for work in probability theory; his papers were in analysis and algebra. That year, he made a significant step in the analysis of the Riemann zeta-function, a topic in complex analysis and number theory at the heart of classical pure mathematics.

Getting statements free from contradictions is the very essence of mathematics. Turing perhaps thought Wittgenstein did not take seriously enough the unobvious and difficult questions that had arisen in the attempt to formalise mathematics; Wittgenstein thought Turing did not take seriously the question of why one should want to formalize mathematics at all.

There are no letters or notes which indicate subsequent contact between Turing and Wittgenstein, and no evidence that Wittgenstein influenced Turing's concept of machines or mind. If influence in the next ten years is sought, it should be found in the Second World War and Turing's amazing part in it.

TRIUMPH OF THE COMPUTER

It is a feature of Turing's thought, one quite untypical of a Cambridge-based mathematician, that his mathematical interests flowed not only into philosophy, but into practical engineering, and with his own generally clumsy hands. The possibilities of machines had seized his imagination. On 14 October 1936 Turing wrote to his mother that

You have often asked me about possible applications of various branches of mathematics. I have just discovered a possible application of the kind of thing I am working on at present. It answers the question 'What is the most general kind of code or cipher possible', and at the same time (rather naturally) enables me to construct a lot of particular and interesting codes. One of them is pretty well impossible to decode without the key, and very quick to encode. I expect I could sell them to H.M. Government for quite a substantial sum, but am rather doubtful about the morality of such things. What do you think?[7]

Nothing more is known about this theoretical investigation, but at Princeton he spent time on building a machine out of electromagnetic relays which effected binary multiplication as an encoding device, with some theory of immunity to cryptananalysis. This Turing machine has not survived, nor has its theory, nor do we know the course of his moral decisions regarding its application. Incidentally, to give the flavour of Turing's personality, he was at this point highly indignant at Baldwin and the British establishment for opposing Edward VIII's marriage. ('As for the Archbishop of Canterbury, I consider his behaviour disgraceful.') However he lost sympathy with the ex-king on learning that he had behaved improperly with state papers. Meanwhile he was an astute judge of the prospect of war with Germany.

When back at Cambridge, Turing also designed and partially built another machine, which approximated by gear-wheel motion a Fourier series for the Riemann zeta-function. It was intended to shorten the hard labour of finding the possible locations of zeros – the subject of the Riemann hypothesis, which remains today perhaps the most important unsolved problem in mathematics. But Turing meanwhile had indicated his interest in cryptography, probably through King's College channels. Whatever the moral and practical means, a rational miracle came about, in which an unworldly person found a perfect application at the heart of the world crisis. In September 1938 he began part-time work on the outstanding problem facing British intelligence: the German Enigma cipher. Progress, however, depended on the Polish mathematicians' work, donated to Britain after the British guarantee to Poland in July 1939. After Hitler called this bluff, Turing began full-time work at Bletchley Park, wartime home of the cryptanalytic establishment.

Turing had substantial influence on the course of the war. In summary: (1) He took on the naval version of Enigma in 1939, when it was thought beyond hope, and found a solution. He said himself that he took up the challenge because 'no-one else was doing anything about it and I could have it to myself.'[8] The reading of U-boat communications, achieved under Turing's direction, was arguably the most vital aspect of Bletchley Park work. (2) Turing crowned the design of the machine (the 'Bombe') which was central to the analysis of all Enigma traffic, with a logical idea which had a curious echo of the discussion with Wittgenstein, as it depended on the flow of logical implications from a false hypothesis. (3) Turing created a theory of information and statistics which made cryptanalysis a scientific subject; he was chief consultant and liaison at the highest level with American work.

Practical work brought with it demands of co-operation and organisation to which Turing was unsuited, and in the early part of the war he had to fight a difficult corner on questions of strategy and resources, at one point joining with other leading analysts to appeal to Churchill over the heads of the administration. But there was another side to this uncongenial coin: war broke peacetime boundaries and gave him practical experience of technology at its leading secret edge. In peace his ideas had flowed into small-scale engineering; in war they led to the electronic digital computer of 1945.

Electronic speeds made a first impact on the Enigma problem in 1942, and thereafter in the engineering of very advanced large-scale Colossus electronic machines for breaking the other high-level German machine cipher, the Lorenz. Note, incidentally, that the Colossus was nothing to do with the Enigma, as is often lazily stated; also that Turing had no part in *designing* the Colossi, but had input into their purpose and saw at first-hand their triumph. Turing did, however, have an electronic design of his own: in 1944, he with one engineer assistant built a speech scrambler of elegant and advanced principle. It appears that in proposing the speech scrambler, not an urgent requirement, he had his own hidden agenda: to acquire electronic experience. The scrambler worked in 1945, and at the same time, Turing combined logic and engineering, pure and applied mathematics, to invent the computer.

Care with words and claims is required: the word 'computer' has changed its meaning. In 1936 and indeed in 1946 it meant a *person* doing computing, and a machine would be called an 'automatic computer'. Until the 1960s people would distinguish digital computers from analogue computers; only since then, as digital computers have swept the field, has the word come to mean a machine such as Turing envisaged. Even now, the word is sometimes applied to any calculating machine. In speaking of 'the computer', I take the salient feature to be that programs and data are alike regarded as symbols which may alike be stored and manipulated – the 'modifiable stored program' – and this is the feature implied by Turing in speaking of a 'practical universal machine', which is how he described his own idea.

Even here, however, care is required. Although the universal machine was presented in 1936 with instructions and working space all in the common form of the 'tape', the instructions only required reading, *not* manipulation or modification, so it would not matter if they were stored in some unalterable physical form. Turing recognized this and counted Babbage's Analytical Engine, on which instructions were fixed cards, as a universal machine. In practice, however, the recognition that programs and data could be stored alike in a symbolic form and could alike be manipulated, was immensely liberating. It made a clean break from the Babbage-like machines which culminated in the electronic ENIAC of 1946. In enunciating the power of the universal machine concept, Turing was far ahead of contemporary wisdom; his idea that a single type of machine could be used for all tasks was stoutly resisted well into the 1950s.

But in peace, Turing's ideas flowed also into philosophy; how did the war affect Turing's philosophy? In *Alan Turing: the Enigma* I wrote that Christopher Morcom had died a second death in 1936, meaning that the concept of spirit freed from Laplacian determinism, which had stimulated Turing in 1930, would never be heard of again. It seemed to me strikingly clear that Turing's emotionally charged fascination with the problem of mind was the key to the mystery of how he, youthful outsider, had made a definitive and fundamental contribution with the concept of computability. By modelling the action of the human mind as a physical machine, he had brought radical new ideas into the world of symbolic logic. After 1936, it seemed, it was the powerful concept of the machine that had seized his imagination; and Turing's post-war writing would support this view. But in fact, his interpretation of ordinal logics in 1938 did leave the door open for something non-mechanical in the mind, and it now seems to me that Turing's views did not shift all at once in 1936 to espouse the total power of the computable.

My guess is that there was a turning point in about 1941. After a bitter struggle to break U-boat Enigma, Turing could then taste triumph. Machines turned and people carried out mechanical methods unthinkingly, with amazing and unforeseen results. This is when there was first talk between Turing and the young I.J. (Jack) Good about chess-playing algorithms. As I described in *Alan Turing: the Enigma*, this vision of mechanical intelligence must have stimulated great excitement; I would now go further and suggest that it was at this period that he abandoned the idea that moments of intuition corresponded to uncomputable operations. Instead, he decided, the scope of the computable encompassed far more than could be captured by explicit instruction notes, and quite enough to include all that human brains did, however creative or original. Machines of sufficient complexity would have the capacity for evolving into behaviour that had never been explicitly programmed. And it was at this period that he also lost interest in logic as a tool for probing reality – although it must be said that he retained a keen interest in theoretical computability *within mathematics*, being one of the first into the field when it was yoked to algebra in the late 1940s.

Possibly it was at the same time, or within months, that he also saw the megahertz speed of electronic components, and their reliable performance in the speech scrambling system used for telephone conversations between Roosevelt and Churchill. I suspect that it was only a short step to see the possibility of building a practical universal Turing machine in electronics. Certainly, by the end of the war, he was captivated by the prospect of exploring the scope of the computable on a universal Turing machine; and indeed he called it 'building a brain' when talking of his plans to his electronic engineer assistant.

Turing went to the National Physical Laboratory and worked on his detailed design for a computer,[9] submitting it for approval in March 1946. Turing's Automatic Computing Engine (ACE), as it was dubbed, was chronologically second to the June 1945 EDVAC report bearing von Neumann's name, but in addition to the originality of its hardware design, it was ideologically independent: for (1) it was conceived from the outset as a universal machine for which arithmetic would be just one application, and (2)

Turing sketched a theory of programming, in which instructions could be manipulated as well as data.

It was an intensely exciting idea that engineering could be done once for all, so that new problems would only need paperwork. Of course, Turing had Bletchley Park as a model of how non-numerical and versatile machines might be urgently needed. Turing dramatised the range of possible operations with farsighted examples, of which the last was as follows:

> Given a position in chess the machine could be made to list all the 'winning combinations' to a depth of about three moves on either side. This is not unlike the previous problem, but raises the question 'Can the machine play chess?' It could fairly easily be made to play a rather bad game. It would be bad because chess requires intelligence. We stated at the beginning of this section [i.e. when describing how programming is done] that the machine should be treated as entirely without intelligence. There are indications however that it is possible to make the machine display intelligence at the risk of its making occasional serious mistakes. By following up this aspect the machine could probably be made to play very good chess.

This is a crucial statement of his thought, which I take to show that by 1945 Turing had come to believe computable operations had sufficient scope to include intelligent behaviour, and had firmly rejected the direction he had followed in studying ordinal logics. The puzzling reference to 'occasional serious mistakes' makes sense in the light of his later stated argument (considered below) for holding uncomputability to be irrelevant to intelligence, and proves that he must have pondered this question during the war.

For a year Turing set forth plans for the practical organisation of a modern computer centre, with a library of routines, and control from remote terminals, exuding the confidence in the collaboration of mathematics, engineering and administration acquired at Bletchley Park. But his plan though formally accepted was not pressed into action; his planned machine (with about 32kbyte storage) was thought far too ambitious. Treated as a liability rather than an asset at the National Physical Laboratory, his eagerness to speak openly of building brains was an embarrassment. In 1947 he left for Cambridge on a 'sabbatical year'.

THE TRAINING OF THOUGHT

During the year, besides training for marathon running to near-Olympic standard, Turing reflected on the 'indications' of mechanical intelligence, writing a report[10] for the National Physical Laboratory in 1948. Cambridge brought about contact with post-war biology; this and contact with 'cybernetic' thinkers probably reinforced his thesis that there was sufficient scope in the complexity of machines to account for apparently non-mechanical behaviour. But Turing's report quoted nothing from such sources; in fact its most conspicuous citation was from a book by, of all people, the religious novelist Dorothy Sayers, which encapsulated the naive notion of 'mechanical' behaviour. (It was a book he was reading in 1941.) And he argued less from biological theory than from his own life experience, in holding that modification of behaviour could be adapted from learning brain to learning machine.

If the untrained infant's mind is to become an intelligent one, it must acquire both discipline and initiative. So far we have been considering only discipline. To convert a brain or machine into a universal machine is the extremest form of discipline. Without something of this kind one cannot set up proper communication. But discipline is certainly not enough in itself to produce intelligence. That which is required in addition we call initiative. This statement will have to serve as a definition. Our task is to discover the nature of this residue ... and to try to copy it in machines.

The influence of the general behaviourist climate seemed to blend easily with his own public school background:

The training of the human child depends largely on a system of rewards and punishments, and this suggests that it ought to be possible to carry through the organising with only two interfering inputs, one for 'pleasure' or 'reward' and the other for 'pain' or 'punishment' ... Pleasure interference has a tendency to fix the character, i.e. towards preventing it changing, whereas pain stimuli tend to disrupt the character, causing features which had become fixed to change ... It is intended that pain stimuli occur when the machine's behaviour is wrong, pleasure stimuli when it is particularly right.

It is often supposed that computers began with heavy arithmetic, and that with this successfully achieved, computer scientists wandered to more ambitious fields. This may be so of others, but is quite untrue of Turing, who had *always* been concerned with modelling the human mind. (Besides, no computer in the modern sense performed a single addition until 1948.) That he now invaded the behavioural sciences is not in itself surprising; more surprising is that he so vehemently embraced the view that apparently non-mechanical steps of 'initiative' were only hidden mechanism, given his own experience of inspiration, and knowledge of the subtlety of computability. I find it surprising also that he used uncritically, almost gleefully, perversely, a primitive view of education. In his actual childhood experience he had ignored social training as much as possible.

Turing's ideas could not be tried out except on a very

small scale as what he called 'paper machines' – the working through of programs by hand. But they anticipated the neural net or connectionist programme of artificial intelligence research, in which what Turing called 'unorganised machines' of sufficient complexity can be trained to perform tasks for which no explicit instructions have ever been written, and where indeed the evolving logical structure is unknown to the human trainer.

His 1948 report, unpublished until 1968, made no impression on the National Physical Laboratory, from which in any case he abruptly resigned. But the ideas resurface, expressed in more general terms, in the famous philosophical paper to which we now turn.

THE TURING TEST

Turing moved to Manchester University, where Newman, professor of pure mathematics there since 1945, had secured for him a first full academic post. Turing had a difficult position as software writer for the pioneer computer, the first such in the world, that the electronic engineer F.C. Williams and his team had built after Newman gave them the principle. Press reports of the machine had already used the terminology of 'brains', which Turing's own comments in 1949 did nothing to discourage. Jefferson, a Manchester brain surgeon, attempted to dispel such talk in a 1949 lecture. Michael Polanyi, chemist turned Christian philosopher of science at Manchester, was another intellectual opponent (with whom, however, Turing was on friendly personal terms). It was probably Polanyi who suggested that Turing should present his views as a paper, which appeared as 'Computing machinery and intelligence' in 1950.[11]

Turing addressed the problem of writing for a non-mathematical readership with typical sang-froid, ignoring all conventional cultural barriers. Notably without any serious citations in philosophical or psychological literature, it stands intransigent in style as well as content.

The paper is now famous for the 'imitation game', as described below, and now often called the Turing test. But the most solid aspect of the paper is Turing's setting out of the model of the *discrete state machine*, which is the Turing machine of 1936, but more clearly thought of as being physically embodied. A careful paragraph explains first why computing machinery is discrete:

> Digital computers . . . may be classified amongst the 'discrete state machines'. These are the machines which move by sudden jumps or clicks from one quite definite state to another. These states are sufficiently different for the possibility of confusion between them to be ignored. Strictly speaking there are no such machines. Everything really moves continuously. But there are many kinds of machine which can profitably be *thought of* as being discrete state machines. For instance in considering the switches for a lighting system it is a convenient fiction that each switch must be definitely on or definitely off. There must be intermediate positions, but for most purposes we can forget about them . . .
>
> This special property of digital computers, that they can mimic any discrete state machine, is described by saying that they are *universal* machines.

Turing's argument is simply that the brain should also be considered as a discrete state machine. In his classic statement, made in a 1952 radio broadcast:[12] 'We are not interested in the fact that the brain has the consistency of cold porridge. We don't want to say, "This machine's quite hard, so it isn't a brain, so it can't think." The physical greyness or soft sponginess of the brain is irrelevant, and so is the mode of operation of the nerves:

> Importance is often attached to the fact that modern

digital computers are electrical, and that the nervous system also is electrical ... Of course electricity usually comes in where fast signalling is concerned, so that it is not surprising that we find it in both these connections. In the nervous system chemical phenomena are at least as important as electrical. In certain computers the storage system is mainly acoustic. The feature of using electricity is thus seen to be only a very superficial similarly. If we wish to find such similarities [i.e. significant similarities between brain and computer] we should look rather for mathematical analogies of function.

Turing's claim is that the only features of the brain relevant to thinking or intelligence are those which fall within the discrete-state-machine level of description. The particular physical embodiment is irrelevant. Not quite made explicit, but implicit in every statement, is that the operation of a discrete state machine is *computable*. We now see the definitive extension to the argument presented in 1936, the effect of the change of thought I conjecture for 1941. The post-war Turing claims that Turing machines can mimic the effect of *any* activity of the mind, not only a mind engaged upon a 'definite method'.

Turing's term 'discrete state machine' is a judicious choice. He avoids expressions such as 'logical structure' which might carry the false connotation of common parlance: logical as opposed to illogical, informal or emotional thought. There is no such dichotomy in Turing's analysis, and indeed no distinction between conscious and unconscious. Turing is clear that discrete state machines include machines with learning or self-organising ability, and makes a point of the fact that these still fall within the scope of the computable. Turing draws attention to the apparant conflict with the definition of Turing machines having fixed tables of behaviour, but sketches a proof that self-modifying machines are still in fact defined by an unchanged instruction set, ending:

The explanation of the paradox is that the rules which get changed in the learning process are of a rather less pretentious kind, claiming only an ephemeral validity. The reader may draw a parallel with the Constitution of the United States.

If Turing's thesis about the function of the brain is accepted, then from a materialist point of view, the argument is almost complete. The behaviour of a discrete state machine can then, at least in principle, be written down in a table. Hence every feature of the brain relevant to thought can be captured by a table of behaviour, and so emulated by a computer. The only question that might remain is that of whether the speed and spatial dimensions of the brain, and the character of its physical interface with the world, are also essential to its function.

However the rest of the paper, bringing in the definition of the Turing test, does much to illustrate the idea of a brain and its function as a physical object whose properties can be examined like any other, and to suggest constructive methods by which intelligent machinery could be engineered. To do this, Turing dramatises the operational viewpoint. Instead of considering the question 'Can machines think?' Turing explains, 'I shall replace the question by another, which is closely related to it and is expressed in relatively unambiguous words':

> The new form of the problem can be described in terms of a game which we call the 'imitation game'. It is played with three people, a man (A), a woman (B), and an interrogator (C) who may be of either sex. The interrogator stays in a room apart from the other two. The object of the game is for the interrogator to determine which of the other two is the man and which is the woman.

If Turing's introduction to the problem of creative mind through a party game with camp innuendo was calculated to offend arts-educated intellectuals, it probably succeeded.

Unfortunately Turing also succeeded in creating disastrous confusion. Although it was intended to clarify the picture of the brain being tested like any other physical object, for many readers the purpose of the imitation game is obscured, in fact turned on its head, by careless syntax:

> We now ask the question, 'What will happen when a machine takes the part of A in this game?' Will the interrogator decide wrongly as often when the game is played like this as he does when the game is played between a man and a woman?

I have no doubt that 'the game is played like this' means, 'the game is played between a human being and a computer pretending to be human'. But many are now the books, articles, lectures, and Webpages which assert that in the Turing test the computer must take the part of a man who is imitating a woman. This is indeed the literal meaning of the words 'a machine takes the part of A', but such an interpretation is contradicted by the sample interrogation:

Q: Please write me a sonnet on the subject of the Forth bridge.
A: Count me out on this one. I never could write poetry.
Q: Add 34957 to 70764.
A: (Pause about 30 seconds and then give as answer) 105621.
Q: Do you play chess?
A: Yes.
Q: I have K at my K1, and no other pieces. You have only K at K6 and R at R1. It is your move, What do you play?
A: (After a pause of 15 seconds) R–R8 mate.

These answers establish no impression of gender; they are meant to establish human intelligence (including – a subtle point – the incorrect addition). The point of the game is this: If a machine cannot be distinguished from a human being under these conditions then we must credit it with human intelligence.

A deeper problem is that Turing's gender-guessing analogy detracts from his own argument. In the gender game, successful fooling of the interrogator proves nothing about the reality behind the screen. In contrast, Turing wants to argue that the successful imitation of intelligence *is* intelligence. Equivalently, Turing defines the subject matter of intelligence as that which can be wholly communicated via the teleprinter link, consistent with his thesis that the brain is relevant only *qua* discrete state machine. Discrete symbols over the teleprinter link can faithfully represent all the inputs and outputs to and from a discrete state machine. As Turing puts it: 'The new problem has the advantage of drawing a fairly sharp line between the physical and intellectual capacities of a man.'

The setting of teleprinter communication is intended to separate intelligence from other faculties of the human being. 'We do not wish to penalise the machine for its inability to shine in beauty competitions, nor to penalise a man for losing in a race against an aeroplane. The conditions of our game make these disabilities irrelevant.' The conditions are intended to make qualities such as gender irrelevant; and from the point of view of clarity it is unfortunate that his iconoclastic introduction gives the opposite impression.

But if Turing's gender-game is misunderstood, he certainly courted such confusion. He painted the pages of this journey into cyberspace with the awkward eroticism and encylopaedic curiosity of his personality. Modern cultural critics have jumped with delight to psychoanalyse its surprises. The intellectual text is the austere statement of the capacity of the discrete state machine for disembodied intelligence; the subtext is full of provocative references to his own person, as if putting his own flesh-and-blood intelligence on trial.

It might be said that the 'imitation' intrinsic to the Turing test is also a distraction from the core of the argument. Subjecting 'imitation' to analysis raises questions, undiscussed in Turing's paper, such as why an intelligent machine should be expected to play a dishonest game; in my view this is overburdening Turing's illustration and missing the main point. The real claim, as I have emphasised above, is that the brain's function is that of a discrete state Turing machine, and therefore can be performed by a computer. The colour and drama in Turing's writing is secondary: it is intended to invite a wide variety of readers into constructive reflection upon this conclusion, which runs contrary to all intuition but is not at all easy to refute.

Courtroom imagery runs through the paper: not only is the Turing test an interrogation, but Turing puts himself in the dock and answers objections to his thesis. The objections differ considerably in how seriously they are set up and taken. After a sally at 'Heads in the Sand' objectors, Turing enunciates:

> *The Theological Objection.* Thinking is a function of man's immortal soul. God has given an immortal soul to every man and woman, but not to any other animal or to machines. Hence no animal or machine can think.

This is not an objection made or answered with seriousness, but used to make fun of Christianity, with a reference to Galileo's heresy as an analogy to his own. He wrote as he spoke: a proud atheist, in the habit of anti-Church remarks. A more serious response might have been aimed not just at religious dogma, but at the more general assertions made by moral philosophy that human beings have properties (e.g. responsibility, authority) that other objects are unable to possess. As it stands, the paragraph might amuse those who already shared his views, it would convince no one who did not. However there is a serious kernel in his debating society point, made to dispose of this objection, that God could give a machine a soul. From the operational viewpoint adopted, Turing need not argue about whether or not people have 'souls'; he need only address what can be observed.

Although rooted in intellectual integrity, there is an unattractiveness in Turing's easy dismissal of such questions. In the aftermath of the Second World War there were good reasons for anxiety about treating people as machines. In his personal attitudes Turing was fierce for liberty and honesty, qualities hard to fit into the setting of the imitation game. But *ad hominem* questions cause one to ask: what words of moral discourse could have been appropriate from an innocent valiant-for-truth who had lent a mastermind to the defeat of Nazism, but could never breathe a word of it? His frivolity had its own moral seriousness, the washing of hands from the evil of the 1940s. Like others of the early 1950s, Turing was impatient to see the future, having defeated Hitler's attempt to destroy it. And with its references to the place of women in Islamic theology, the cloning of human beings, and the question of animals' consciousness, one cannot accuse Turing's paper of lacking foresight for moral issues.

I now turn to the strangest passage in all Turing's writing.

The Argument from Extra-Sensory Perception. I assume that the reader is familiar with the idea of extra-sensory perception, and the meaning of the four items of it, *viz.* telepathy, clairvoyance, precognition and psycho-kinesis. These disturbing phenomena seem to deny all our usual scientific ideas. How we should like to discredit them! Unfortunately the statistical evidence, at least for telepathy, is overwhelming. It is very difficult to rearrange one's ideas so as to fit these new facts in. Once one has accepted them it does not seem a very big step to believe in ghosts and bogies. The idea that our bodies move simply according to the known laws of physics, together with some others not yet discovered but somewhat similar, would be one of the first to go.

This argument is to my mind quite a strong one. One can say in reply that many scientific theories seem to remain workable in practice, in spite of clashing with E.S.P.; that in fact one can get along very nicely if one forgets about it. This is rather cold comfort, and one fears that thinking is just the kind of phenomenon where E.S.P. may be especially relevant.

It is not clear how serious the statements are. The exclamation mark suggests irony, the 'overwhelming' evidence sounds literal. On balance it appears he was at that time convinced by contemporary claims for observing ESP. There are no other passages on ESP in Turing's writing or letters, although his interest in dreams and strange events was sharp. In 1930 he had a presentiment of Christopher Morcom's death at the very moment he was taken ill, and he later wrote, 'It is not difficult to explain these things away – but, I wonder!' He wondered; it was natural wonder.

There is a point made here, though left elliptical, of more general significance: namely that the discrete state machine model rests upon the brain's operation according to 'known laws of physics, together with some others not yet discovered but somewhat similar'; we shall return to this question.

Further objections are more clearly made and seriously answered, and of these I consider first what Turing called:

The Argument from Consciousness: This argument is very well expressed in Professor Jefferson's Lister Oration for 1949 ... 'Not until a machine can write a sonnet or compose a concerto because of thoughts and emotions felt, and not by the chance fall of symbols, could we agree that machine equals brain – that is, not only write it but know that it had written it. No mechanism could feel (and not merely artificially signal, an easy contrivance) pleasure at its successes, grief when its valves fuse, be warmed by flattery, be made miserable by its mistakes, be charmed by sex, be angry or depressed when it cannot get what it wants.'

This argument appears to be a denial of the validity of our test. According to the most extreme form of this view the only way by which one could be sure that a machine thinks is to *be* the machine and to feel oneself thinking. One could then describe these feelings to the world, but of course no one would be justified in taking any notice. Likewise according to this view the only way to know what a *man* thinks is to be that particular man. It is in fact the solipsist point of view ...

I do not wish to give the impression that I think there is no mystery about consciousness. There is, for instance, something of a paradox connected with any attempt to localise it. But I do not think these mysteries necessarily need to be solved before we can answer the question with which we are concerned in this paper.

Jefferson's central objection is that of commonsense repugnance to the idea of machines being credited with thought; and its burden is similar to John Searle's claim of the machine lacking human 'intentionality'. It is of interest, even if anachronistic, to guess Turing's answer to Searle's parable of the Chinese Room, itself a sort of riposte to the drama of the imitation game. Searle supposes (1) That there is an algorithm for translating Chinese to English; (2) that this algorithm is effected not by a machine but by one or many people in a room, working mindlessly. Then the Chinese is translated; but none of the translators has the faintest knowledge or understanding: a paradox. Turing's thesis is, I believe, that this if achieved would be no paradox at all, merely a dramatisation of the true state of affairs. It would reflect the mechanism of the brain, where the neurones have no understanding individually, but somehow the system as a whole seems to; and that appearance is all that matters. One might go further: the situation in Bletchley Park was uncannily like the Chinese Room, since for reasons of secrecy people were trained to perform the cryptanalytic algorithms without knowing their purpose. Perhaps this very sight, of good judgement emerging from mindless calculation, was what positively inspired Turing to the picture of mechanical intelligence in about 1941. The drift of Turing's views is that the definiteness of consciousness is an illusion, a quality emerging from and ultimately to be explained by great complexity. His approach would not accept 'intentionality' as any better an explanation than 'soul'. For a materialist such words are a restatement of the problem, perhaps the greatest problem of science, and not an answer to it.

At this point it is appropriate to introduce the ideas of Roger Penrose, who shares the materialist dissatisfaction with explanations through souls or intentionality, but holds consciousness to be an undeniable fact. Penrose poses a physical question about consciousness, probably similar to what Turing had in mind when referring to a paradox in trying to localise it: is the intelligence supposed to emerge when the machine is run? If so, it is not the discrete state machine alone, but that *plus* its physical implementation. Or is intelligence present in the abstract table of behaviour? But if so, we could choose a notation where the number 42 encodes the table of behaviour of Einstein's brain; can 42 have Einstein's intelligence? As Turing says, his own presentation leaves such mysteries unresolved.

Turing's most positive contribution comes as a response to what he called:

Lady Lovelace's Objection. Our most detailed information of Babbage's Analytical Engine comes from a memoir by Lady Lovelace. In it she states, 'The Analytical Engine has no pretentions to *originate* anything. It can do *whatever we know how to order it* to perform.'

This is the cue for a large section on learning machines, with constructive arguments for how machines might do apparently unmechanical things for which explicit programs are unknown: the first public exposition of what I have called his 1941 vision. Turing advocates two different approaches – in modern parlance top-down and bottom-up – which in fact derive from his 1936 descriptions of the machine model. Explicit instruction notes become explicit progamming; implicit states of mind become the states of machines attained by learning and self-organizing experience. Turing's positive assurance that machines are capable of all that anyone including himself had done, is illustrated in curiously masochistic self-deprecation, and one passage has a particular resonance:

> The view that machines cannot give rise to surprises is due, I believe, to a fallacy to which philosophers and mathematicians are particularly subject. This is the assumption that as soon as a fact is presented to a mind all consequences of that fact spring into the mind simultaneously with it. It is a very useful assumption under many circumstances, but one too easily forgets that it is false. A natural consequence of doing so is that one then assumes that there is no virtue in the mere working out of consequences from data and general principles.

Turing could hardly have typed these words without private allusion to his own contribution ten years earlier, in another world: for his logical breakthrough into the Enigma involved the instantaneous flow of implications, as embodied in ingenious electrical circuitry. He was crediting the mechanical with the capacity for everything, including moments of world-shattering inspiration.

I come now to a raft of questions which arise through the question of how the brain interacts with the external world. Some of these Turing discusses under Jefferson's objections; others fall under 'The argument from disabilities'.

The inability to enjoy strawberries and cream may have

struck the reader as frivolous. Possibly a machine might be made to enjoy this delicious dish, but any attempt to make one to do so would be idiotic. What is important about this disability is that it contributes to some of the other disabilities, *e.g.* to the difficulty of the same kind of friendliness occurring between man and machine as between white man and white man, or between black man and black man.

Just as the themes of moral philosophy are hardly met by Turing's theological response, these are somewhat throwaway remarks with which to dispose of the entire content of the social sciences, in which thought and behaviour are considered dominated by external influence. But this was not because Turing was sure of his ground in this case; rather, it is on topics involving interaction that Turing shows himself least certain, anxious about what sensory and motor organs an artificial brain will require. In the development of his thought away from the mathematical calculations of 1936, he allowed first chess, cryptography and (tentatively) languages in the 1948 report as 'topics where not too much interaction is required'. His reference to the machine being denied 'sex, sport and other things of interest to the human being' must have struck an unusual note in the archives of the National Physical Laboratory, and again in the 1948 report Turing distinguishes the concentrating and non-interacting brain from the process of interaction which allows it to learn:

> We may say then that in so far as a man is a machine he is one that is subject to very much interference ... constantly receiving visual and other stimuli ... it is important to remember that although a man when concentrating may behave like a machine without interference, his behaviour when concentrating is largely determined by the way he has been conditioned by previous interference.

Unless the intellectual and physical, internal and external, can be separated, the value of the discrete state machine model of the brain is questionable, for the interface with the ambient world becomes crucial, and the robotic elements need attention as well as the simulation of brain function. In the 1950 paper Turing finally loses all inhibition and throws open the machine to general conversation, but the problem of physical interaction is still an anxiety:

> Instead of trying to produce a programme to simulate the adult's mind, why not rather try to produce one which simulates the child's? ... It will not be possible to apply exactly the same teaching process to the machine as to a normal child. It will not, for instance, be provided with legs, so that it could not be asked to go out and fill the coal scuttle. Possibly it might not have eyes. But however well these deficiencies might be overcome by clever engineering, we could not send the creature to school without the other children making excessive fun of it. It must be given some tuition. We need not be too concerned about the legs, eyes, etc. The example of Miss Helen Keller shows that education can take place ...

These are untypical worries for a mathematician, but then Turing was more natural philosopher than typical mathematician, and the connection between thinking and doing was what had inspired his Turing machine construction in the first place.

> We may hope that machines will eventually compete with men in all purely intellectual fields. But which are the best ones to start with? ... Many people think that a very abstract activity, like the playing of chess, would be best. It can also be maintained that it is best to provide the machine with the best sense organs that money can buy, and then teach it to understand and speak English ... Again I do not know what the right answer is, but I think both approaches should be tried.

THE UNCOMPUTABLE REVISITED

The remaining questions concern the computable discrete state machine model itself, and are the most fundamental. Turing points out that in a theoretical discrete state machine:

> It will seem that given the initial state of the machine and the input signals it is always possible to predict all future states. This is reminiscent of Laplace's view that from the complete state of the universe at one moment of time, as described by the positions and velocities of all particles, it should be possible to predict all future states. The prediction which we are considering is, however, rather nearer to practicability than that considered by Laplace. The system of the 'universe as a whole' is such that quite small errors in the initial conditions can have an overwhelming effect at a later time. The displacement of a single electron by a billionth of a centimetre at one moment might make the difference between a man being killed by an avalanche a year later, or escaping. It is an essential property of the mechanical systems which we have called 'discrete state machines' that this phenomenon does not occur.

This perhaps needs clarification: Turing means that the small physical displacement of an electron inside a computer will not (except with an extremely small probability) affect the discrete state that the computer is representing. Hence it will not affect the future evolution of the computation.

On this basis, Turing then poses

The Argument from Continuity in the Nervous System: The nervous system is certainly not a discrete-state machine. A small error in the information about the size of a nervous impulse impinging on a neuron, may make a large difference to the size of the outgoing impulse. It may be argued that, this being so, one cannot expect to be able to mimic the behaviour of the nervous system with a discrete-state system.

Turing's following remarks briefly indicate how a digital machine can imitate analogue machines, so that discreteness would be no disadvantage. On this topic, Penrose has reinforced Turing's comment, with the observation that 'avalanche' effects of instability and amplification, nowadays better understood through the analysis of chaos, are to the *brain*'s disadvantage, and no argument against the feasibility of machine intelligence.

But this brings us to Penrose's central objection, which is not to the *discreteness* of Turing's machine model of the brain, but to its *computability*. Penrose holds that the function of the brain must have evolved by purely physical processes, but that its behaviour is – in fact must be – *uncomputable*. Since it cannot be that the laws of Nature are waived for the atoms in the brain, it follows that physical law, which at present is incompletely known, must in general have non-computable aspects. Penrose sees the key in the as yet unknown rules which govern the reduction of the wave function in quantum mechanics. Turing raises no such possibility, and if we look for a discussion of what physical laws he supposes to underpin the function of the brain, we find a vagueness that is surprising considering Turing's knowledge of applied mathematics and physical theory. Apart from the remark made on ESP (raising the possibility of laws of physics different from those so far known) there is only a comment that, 'Even when we consider the actual physical machines instead of the idealised machines, reasonably accurate knowledge of the state at one moment yields reasonably accurate knowledge any number of steps later.' This can be elucidated by reference to his 1948 report; it refers *not* to quantum mechanics but to uncertainty in classical thermodynamics. The tendency of Turing's argument, though not explicitly stated, is that once the discrete state machine model is arrived at, it does not matter what exactly physical laws are. However, the ESP discussion does implicitly admit that physical law enters into the underlying assumptions. Penrose takes a completely different point of view: to discuss what the mind does, as Turing attempts, it is of prime importance to know the fundamental physical content of mental 'doing'. But fundamental physics is quantum-mechanical and at present not fully known; here according to Penrose must lie a fundamental non-computability in nature, which the brain has evolved to take advantage of.

Quite apart from Penrose's theory, it is unclear how to apply computability to continuous quantities, as Turing must have known since he had to abandon in 1937 his intention of rewriting continuous analysis. The question of the computability of physical laws, which are generally expressed as differential equations for continuous variables, remains a loose end in Turing's argument.

With computability now at the forefront, it is worth a further look at the problems of interaction between brain and external world. From Penrose's point of view these are irrelevant. If the physical world is computable, then in principle the world external to a brain can be simulated by a computer, and so all its experiences could be faithfully imitated; hence all interface questions take second place to the question of the computability of physical law. The same view is adopted by the most confident proponents of artifical intelligence, though with the opposite intent: they are happy to conceive of simulating the whole external world as well as a single brain. Turing never suggests doing this, but imagines a machine learning from interaction with the world; here his anxieties are concentrated. Penrose, regarding these problems as irrelevant, focuses attention on those questions of intelligence in which external interaction plays no role, questions in pure mathematics. In Penrose's view the impossibility of mechanical intelligence can be seen within mathematics alone: and this impossibility can be put in terms of Turing's own uncomputable numbers. How did Turing himself deal with this objection?

As I have already suggested, Turing probably decided in the 1941 period that the uncomputable, unprovable and undecidable were irrelevant to the problem of mind. In the 1950 paper, Turing exposes and responds to what he calls 'the mathematical objection', but his answer is short, and I therefore quote the fuller version he gave in a talk to mathematicians in 1947:

> It has for instance been shown that with certain logical systems there can be no machine which will distinguish provable formulae of the system from unprovable, i.e. that there is no test that the machine can apply which will divide propositions with certainty into these two classes. Thus if a machine is made for this purpose it must in some cases fail to give an answer. On the other hand if a mathematician is confronted with such a problem he would search around and find new methods of proof, so that he ought to be able to reach a decision about any given formula. This would be the argument. Against it I would say that fair play must be given to the machine. Instead of it sometimes giving no answer we could arrange that it gives occasional wrong answers. But the human mathematician would likewise make blunders when trying out new techniques. It is easy for us to regard these blunders as not counting and give him another chance, but the machine would probably be allowed no mercy. In other words, then, if a machine is expected to be infallible, it cannot also be intelligent.[13]

This is the passage which explains the 1946 ACE report claim for the 'indications' of machine intelligence at the cost of making serious mistakes. Penrose disputes Turing's argument: we do not expect intelligence in mathematics to turn upon the making of mistakes, and even if a result is mistaken, it can be reliably verified or corrected by others when communicated. Indeed the very essence of mathematical intelligence is *seeing the truth*. In the 1950 paper, Turing adds a further statement, again very brief: 'There would be no question of triumphing simultaneously over *all* machines. In short, then, there might be men cleverer than any given machine, but then again there might be other machines cleverer again, and so on.' This may be contrasted with Penrose's explicit and detailed exposition of human triumph over any Turing machine capable of partial judgements on the halting problem by an argument that is a development of seeing the truth of unprovable Gödel statements. This, in Penrose's argument, establishes that the mind is capable of the uncomputable. Turing's bald assertion, putting human and machine on a par, is no more than reassertion of his claim that the brain's function is that of a discrete state machine; it does not add any evidential weight to it.

So in the course of the war Turing dismissed the role for uncomputability in the description of mind, which once he had cautiously explored with the ordinal logics. A great body of opinion has followed Turing's example; not only within computer science, but in philosophy and the cognitive sciences. To a surprising degree the subject of mathematical logic, in Russell's time an enquiry into fundamental truth, has followed Turing's example and come to justify itself as adjunct to computer science. Yet Turing was careful to offer his conclusions not as dogma, but as constructive conjectures to be tested by scientific investigation.

I believe that in about fifty years' time it will be possible to programme computers, with a storage capacity of about 10^9, to make them play the imitation game so well that an average interrogator will not have more than 70 per cent chance of making the right identification after five minutes of questioning. The original question, 'Can machines think?' I believe to be too meaningless to deserve discussion. Nevertheless I believe that at the end of the century the use of words and general educated opinion will have altered so much that one will be able to speak of machines thinking without expecting to be contradicted. I believe further that no useful purpose is served by concealing these beliefs. The popular view that scientists proceed inexorably from well-established fact to well-established fact, never being influenced by any unproved conjecture, is quite mistaken. Provided it is made clear which are proved facts and which are conjectures, no harm can result. Conjectures are of great importance since they suggest useful lines of research.

A notable feature of the Turing test setting is that it requires not so much a judge as a jury: not an expert, but common humanity. The democracy of Turing's thought has lasted well. As new computer applications come into circulation, the technology of the Internet will give a new spin to the futuristic drama of the Turing test. We shall all judge for ourselves.

The fifty-year figure seems to derive from an estimate of sixty people working fifty years to write sufficient code: hardly a practical research proposal, and indeed no such proposal was made. In July 1951 Turing gained the use of a more reliable machine at Manchester, but there is no trace of him using it to simulate neural networks, nor to code chess-playing algorithms. He and the small group around him published articles[14] under the heading 'Digital computers applied to games' in 1953, which mark pioneering research into machine intelligence. But this lead made no impact on the fresh start to artificial intelligence made by Newell, Simon, Minsky and McCarthy in the United States. Turing never wrote the book on theory and practice of computation which would have established his reputation. Nor was he prepared to argue and fight over strategy and practical support: he had done this successfully in 1940 over naval Enigma, he had done it unsuccessfully in 1946 for the ACE; after this he did not try again.

GROWING CRISIS

In any case, by 1950 Turing had an excited interest in a new field. Turing was interested in the body in Nature as well as the brain; his boyhood experiments had been chemical rather than mathematical, he retained the eyes to see biological structure as intensely puzzling. We recall his early fascination with determinism and his idea that 'the rest of the body amplifies' the action of the brain. His later claims for machine intelligence and the mechanical simulation of learning had directed his attention to the growth of brain cells. He now formulated some simplified problems in biological growth, and attacked them by postulating non-linear differential chemical equations. He showed how inhomogeneity could arise from homogeneous initial conditions, using a symmetry-breaking effect of chemical instability.[15] He described his philosophical outlook as countering the theological argument from design, suggesting a future Richard Dawkins of physiology. He set himself as a goal the explanation of Fibonacci patterns in plants; this was perhaps unfortunate as this problem remains unsolved, but his research, as a first user of electronic computation for serious mathematical investigation, was twenty years ahead of its time and full of potential for discovery. With hindsight we notice that the elucidation of chaotic dynamics was later to come from just such computational experiment.

This work struggled against personal catastrophe. In December 1951 he met a young man in Manchester, and told him of his work on 'the electronic brain'. An unsatisfactory affair led to indirect blackmail, exploiting the fact that all sex between men was then criminal. Resisting it by going to the police, he was arrested. Unrepentant and unashamed at his trial, he had to agree to the injection of oestrogen, supposed to neutralize his supposedly unnatural nature. The alternative would have been prison. Deemed a security risk by post-war regulations, he was stopped from the work he had continued to do from GCHQ, the Cold War successor to Bletchley Park. He found himself under watch; and other pressures may have been placed on him.

Turing complained that he lacked concentration; yet for two years he developed a mass of geometric and analytic-ideas; he also turned to new topics, or rather old ones revived. In particular, he puzzled over the standard view of reduction of the wave-function in quantum mechanics, noting the paradox that continous observation freezes the dynamics. He told Robin Gandy of his new idea for quantum mechanics: 'Description must be non-linear, prediction must be linear.'[16] Possibly he had in mind a non-linear quantum theory in which reduction would arise as did the symmetry breaking in his non-linear morphogenetic theory.

To relieve depression and anger he had turned to Jungian therapy, and found new interest in writing down his dreams. On a visit to Blackpool in early 1954 with the therapist's family, he consulted the Gypsy Queen fortune-teller, and emerged 'white as a sheet'. He remained silent for the rest of that day; nor did he leave a public word at his suicide on Whit Monday, 7 June 1954. Symbolism, in the cyanide-poisoned apple he ate, was his language. What words could have sufficed? Jokes, as perhaps in the 1950 paper, were his serious defence from the ineffable irony of the world. After his arrest he wrote:

> Turing believes machines think
> Turing lies with men
> Therefore machines do not think [17]

and shortly before he died, he wrote postcards headed 'Messages from the Unseen World' – explicitly referring to

Eddington, some with schoolboy allusions, and a hymn-like relativistic verse:

> Hyperboloids of wondrous Light
> Rolling for aye through space and time
> Harbour those waves which somehow might
> Play out God's holy pantomime.[18]

Had an earlier agenda, the nature of spirit, resurfaced? Would he have reconsidered his philosophy, bringing quantum mechanical substrate into the discrete-state picture? In my biography I suggested that the emotional intensity and gross interference of this period might have undermined his certainty in the mechanical model of mind, but offered no evidence, for there is none. His last publication[19] was in *Penguin Science News*, written like a modern *Scientific American* article, and entitled 'Solvable and unsolvable problems'. Written vividly but from the perspective of a pure mathematician, its final words concerned the interpretation of unsolvable problems, such as the halting problem for Turing machines. They were lame: 'These … may be regarded as going some way towards a demonstration, within mathematics itself, of the inadequacy of "reason" unsupported by common sense.' No clues are offered here.

Alan Turing's philosophy might appear the ultimate in reductionism, in its atomising of mental process, its scorn for the non-material. Yet it depends upon a synthesis of vision running against the grain of an intellectual world split into many verbal or mathematical or technical specialisms. He preached the computable, but never lost natural wonder; the law killed and the spirit gave life.

NOTES

1. Letter to Turing's mother, Mrs E. Sara Turing, now in the Turing Archive at King's College, Cambridge.

2. *Nature of Spirit*, Turing's undated manuscript, is in the King's College Archive. Full text in *Alan Turing: the Enigma* (see below).

3. A.M. Turing, 'On computable numbers, with an application to the Entscheidungsproblem', Proc. Lond. Math. Soc. ser. 2, 42 (1936–7) pp. 230–65; correction ibid. 43 (1937) pp. 544–6. The paper is not yet available in the *Collected Works*, but is reprinted in Martin Davis (ed.), *The Undecidable* (Raven Press, New York, 1965).

4. A.M. Turing, 'Systems of logic based on ordinals', Proc. Lond. Math. Soc. ser. 2, 45 (1939) pp. 161–228. The paper is not yet available in the *Collected Works*, but is reprinted in *The Undecidable*.

5. Ibid.

6. C. Diamond (ed.), *Wittgenstein's Lectures on the Foundations of Mathematics* (Harvester Press, 1976). The quoted dialogue is extracted from lectures 21 and 22.

7. Letter to E. S. Turing, in the Turing Archive, King's College, Cambridge.

8. A.P. Mahon, *History of Hut 8* (1945), released from secrecy by the National Archives, Washington DC, April 1996.

9. A.M. Turing, 'Proposed Electronic Calculator', National Physical Laboratory report (1946). Published in B.E. Carpenter and R.W. Doran (eds.), *A.M. Turing's ACE Report of 1946 and other papers* (MIT Press and Tomash Publishers, 1986); and again in the *Collected Works*.

10. A.M. Turing, 'Intelligent machinery', National Physical Laboratory report (1948). The edition (by D. Michie) in *Machine Intelligence*, 5 (1969) pp. 3–23 has been reproduced in the *Collected Works*.

11. A.M. Turing, 'Computing machinery and intelligence', Mind, 51 (1950), pp. 433–60; reprinted in the *Collected Works*.

12. Transcript, in the Turing Archive, King's College, Cambridge, published in the MIT Press volume (see 9, above- and again in the *Collected Works*.

14. B.V. Bowden (ed.) *Faster than Thought* (Pitman, 1953). Turing contributed the section on chess (pp. 288–95), which is reprinted in the *Collected Works*.

15. A.M. Turing, 'The chemical basis of morphogenesis', Phil. Trans. R. Soc. London B 237 (1952) pp. 37–72; reprinted in the *Collected Works*.

16. Letter of June 1954 from Robin Gandy to M.H.A. Newman, in the Turing Archive, King's College, Cambridge.

17. Letter to N.A. Routledge, in the Turing Archive, King's College, Cambridge. Reprinted in the preface to the 1992 edition of *Alan Turing: the Enigma*.

18. Postcard to Robin Gandy, in the Turing Archive, King's College, Cambridge. Reproduced in *Alan Turing: the Enigma*.

19. A.M. Turing, 'Solvable and unsolvable problems', *Penguin Science News*, 31 (1954), pp. 7–23. Reprinted in the *Collected Works*.

THE COLLECTED WORKS

J.L. Britton, D.C. Ince, P.T. Saunders (eds), *Collected Works of A.M. Turing* (Elsevier, 1992).

Three volumes have appeared, with extensive annotation by the editors. The fourth, containing Turing's papers in mathematical logic (eds. R.O. Gandy and C.E.M. Yates) is still (as at 1997) in preparation.

STARTING-POINTS FOR FURTHER READING

Herken, Rolf, (ed.), *The Universal Turing Machine* (Oxford University Press, 1988), includes definitive articles on the concept of computability.

Hinsley, F. H. and Alan Stripp (eds.), *Codebreakers, The Inside Story of Bletchley Park* (Oxford University Press, 1993).

Hodges, Andrew, *Alan Turing: the Enigma* (London, Burnett with Hutchinson, 1983; New York, Simon & Schuster, 1983; new edn. London, Vintage, 1992)

Hodges, Andrew, *http://www.turing.org.uk/turing/Turing.html* Website with updates of information and comment, bibliography, links, images, and Turing machines.

Millican, P.J.R., and A. Clark (eds.), *Machines and Thought: the Legacy of Alan Turing* (Oxford, Clarendon Press, 1996).

Penrose, Roger, 'Beyond the doubting of a shadow' (*Psyche*, electronic journal, 1996: *http://psyche.cs.monash.edu.au/volume2–1/psyche-96-2-23-shadows-10-penrose.html*) is the best introduction to the ideas developed in Penrose's *The Emperor's New Mind* (Oxford University Press, 1989) and *Shadows of the Mind* (Oxford University Press, 1994).